One Little Slip

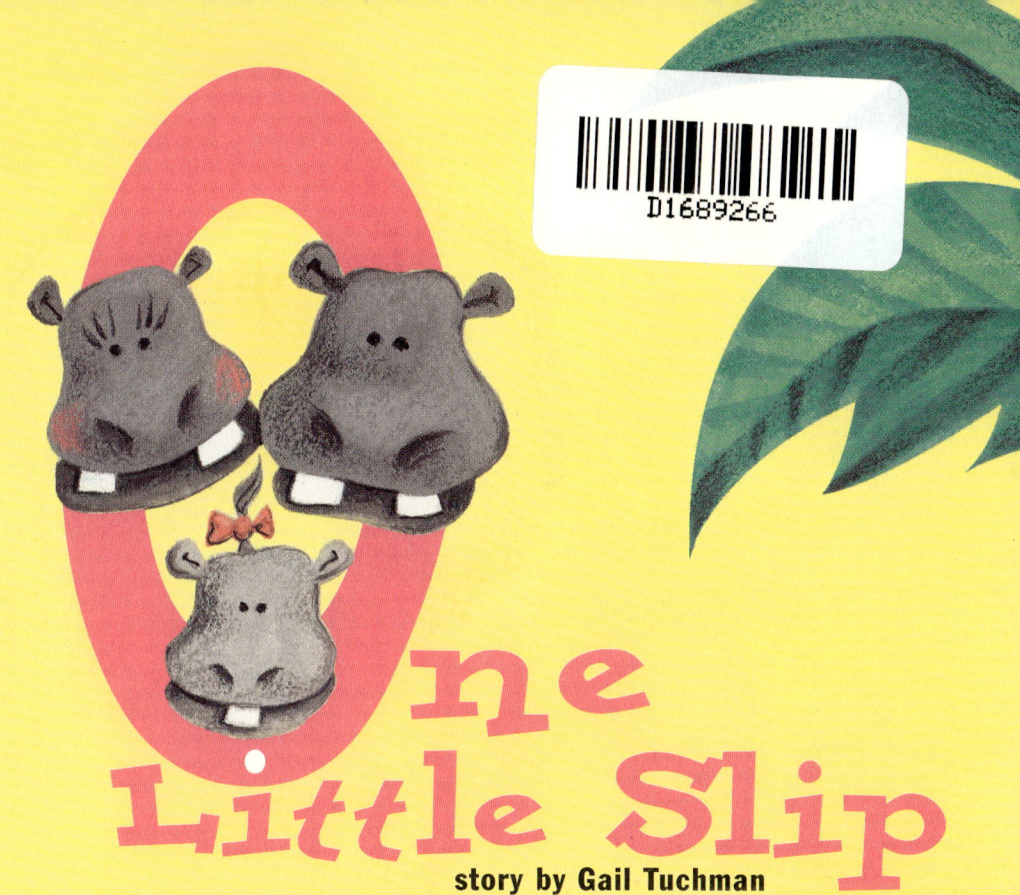

story by Gail Tuchman
illustrations by Gerald McDermott

HARCOURT BRACE & COMPANY

Orlando Atlanta Austin Boston San Francisco Chicago Dallas New York
Toronto London

When Little Hippo took a trip,

she began to slip.

When Mother Hippo took a flip,

she began to dip.

When Father Hippo took a sip,

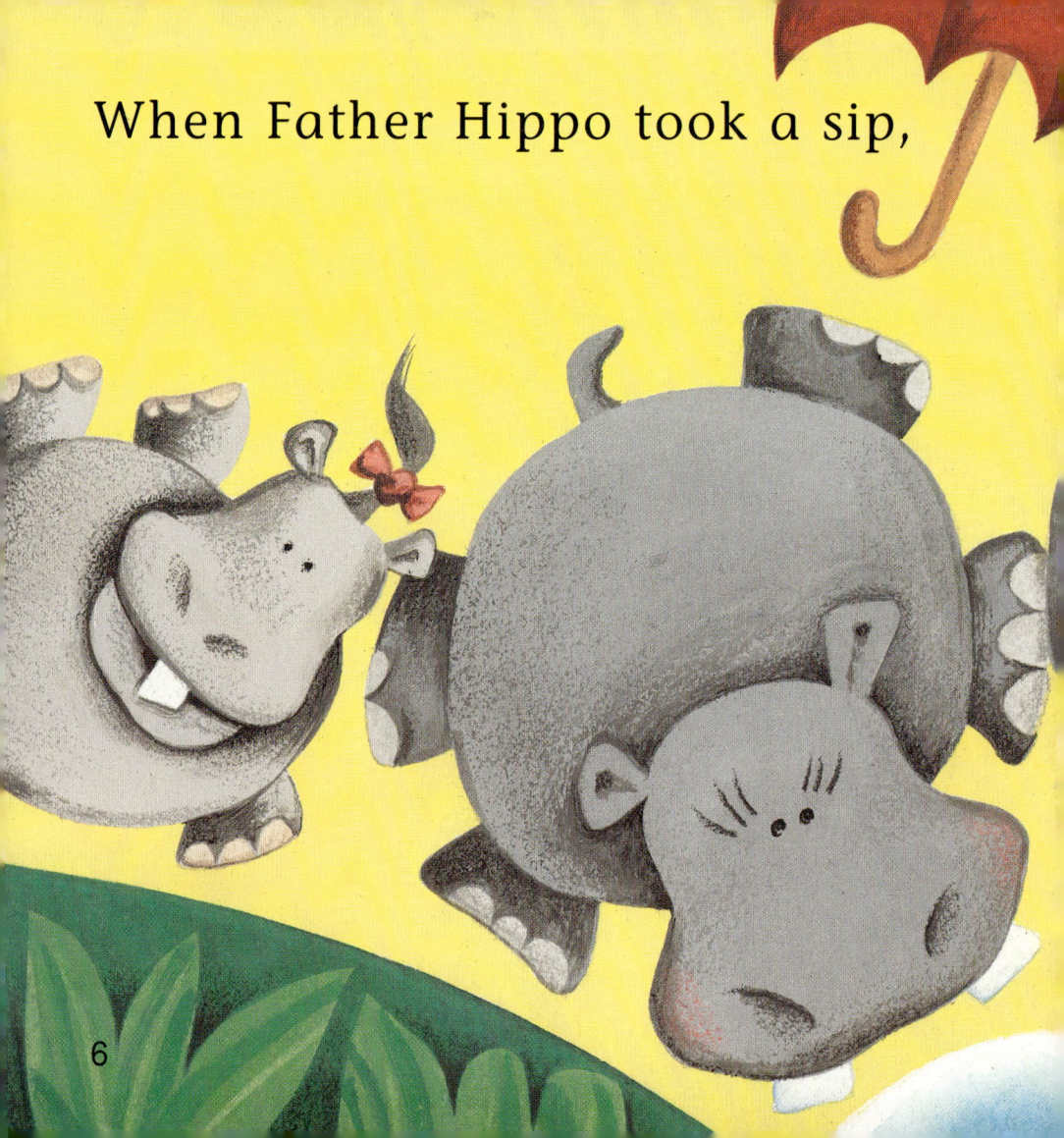

he began to tip.

Drip,
   drip,
      drip.